AMV

ACPL ITEM
DISCARDED
CIRCULATING WITH THE LISTED PROBLEM(S):

Msg. pages 33-34
SP 9/03

D1616520

Project Manager: CAROL CUELLAR
BookArt Layout: LISA GREENE MANE

2000 ZOMBA RECORDING CORP.

© 2000 WARNER BROS. PUBLICATIONS
All Rights Reserved

Any duplication, adaptation or arrangement of the compositions
contained in this collection requires the written consent of the Publisher.
No part of this book may be photocopied or reproduced in any way without permission.
Unauthorized uses are an infringement of the U.S. Copyright Act and are punishable by law.

JUSTIN
TIMBERLAKE

LANCE
BASS

JC
CHASEZ

JOEY
FATONE

CHRIS
KIRKPATRICK

SPACE COWBOY (YIPPIE-YI-YAY)
(featuring Lisa "Left Eye" Lopes)

Moderate funk ♩ = 112

Words and Music by
JC CHASEZ, ALEX GREGGS, BRADLEY DAYMOND,
LISA LOPES and INGA WILLIS

Spoken: (Riprock, AG, come in, over. Yo, turn me up, I wanna be heard.
See, I'm talkin' about the future, y'all, and the future looks bright, 'specially when we rip it in half.)

Verse:

1. Here it comes, mil-len-ni-um, and
2. See additional lyrics

ev-'ry-bod-y's talk-in' 'bout Je-ru-sa-lem.___ Is this the be-gin-ning or be-

Space Cowboy - 7 - 1
PFM0021

© 2000 ZOMBA ENTERPRISES INC., CHASEZ MUSIC, ALEX GREGGS PUBLISHING,
BMG MUSIC PUBLISHING CANADA INC. and INTERNASH SONGS
All Rights on behalf of CHASEZ MUSIC and ALEX GREGGS PUBLISHING Administered by ZOMBA ENTERPRISES INC. (ASCAP)
All Rights Reserved

Lyrics:
gin-ning of the end? Well, I've got oth-er thoughts, my friend._____ See,

I've got my eyes__ on the skies,____ the heav-en-ly bod-ies up high,__

_____ and if you're in the mood to take a ride,_____ then

strap on__ a suit____ and get__ in - side._____

3 1833 03782 3603

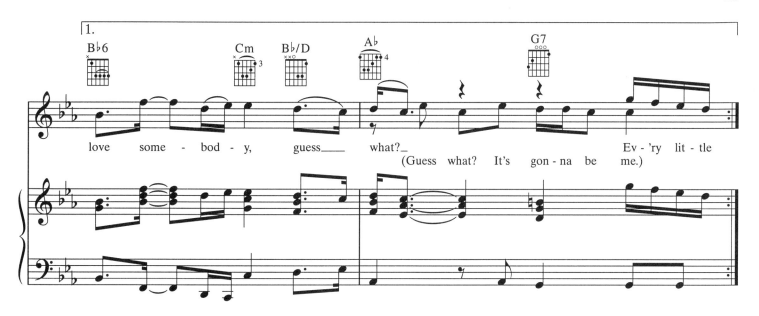

love some-bod-y, guess____ what?__
(Guess what? It's gon-na be me.)
Ev-'ry lit-tle

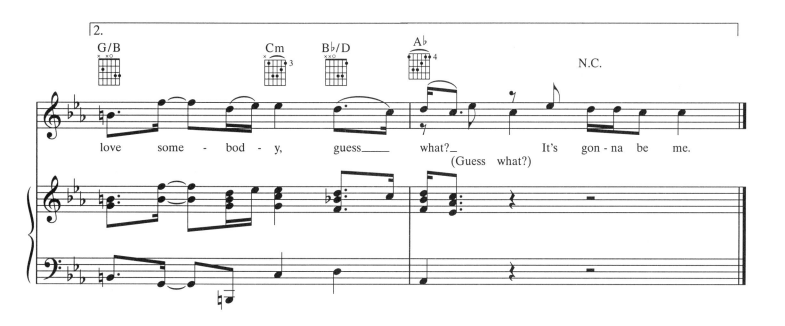

love some-bod-y, guess____ what?__ It's gon-na be me.
(Guess what?)

Verse 2:
You've got no choice, babe,
But to move on, you know
There ain't no time to waste,
'Cause you're just too blind to see.
But in the end you know it's gonna be me.
You can't deny,
So just tell me why…
(To Chorus:)

JUST GOT PAID

Words and Music by
TEDDY RILEY, GENE GRIFFIN,
AARON HALL and JOHNNY KEMP

© 1990 ZOMBA ENTERPRISES INC., DONRIL MUSIC, EMI VIRGIN SONGS for itself and CAL–GENE MUSIC,
VIRGIN MUSIC CAL–ROCK, EMI APRIL MUSIC INC. and MOCHRIE MUSIC
All Rights on behalf of DONRIL MUSIC Administered by ZOMBA ENTERPRISES INC. (ASCAP)
All Rights Reserved

Bridge:

Verse 2:
On the floor, rockin' to the beat,
Always sure look sweet.
Fine young lady, standing by,
Come on, baby, sweet, eye delight.
I love the way that you move,
You look so sweet when you're movin' to the beat.
I'm tired of all these boring parties, baby.
Why can't we get on down?
Let's get on down!
(To Chorus:)

36

This I Promise You - 5 - 4
PFM0021

IT MAKES ME ILL

Words and Music by
KEVIN BRIGGS and KANDI BURRUSS

Moderately ♩ = 104

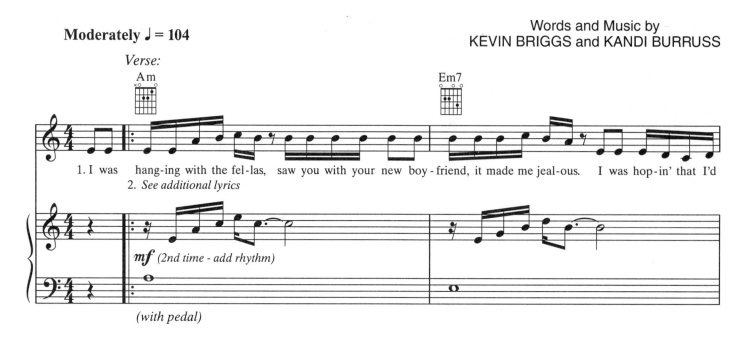

1. I was hang-ing with the fel-las, saw you with your new boy-friend, it made me jeal-ous. I was hop-in' that I'd
2. *See additional lyrics*

mf (2nd time - add rhythm)

(with pedal)

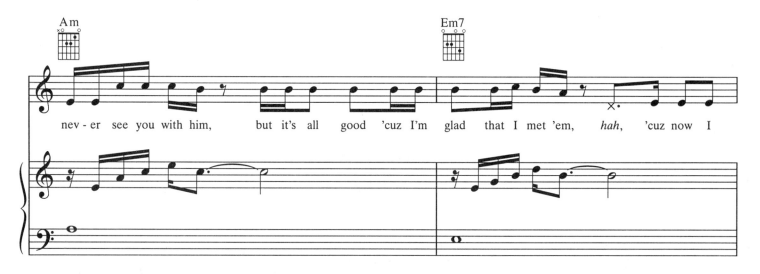

nev-er see you with him, but it's all good 'cuz I'm glad that I met 'em, *hah,* 'cuz now I

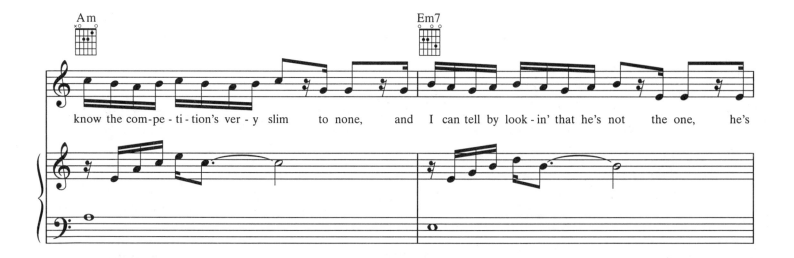

know the com-pe-ti-tion's ver-y slim to none, and I can tell by look-in' that he's not the one, he's

© 2000 MUSIC OF WINDSWEPT on behalf of HITCO SOUTH and SHEK'EM DOWN MUSIC,
KANDACY MUSIC INC., AIR CONTROL MUSIC, INC. and EMI APRIL MUSIC, INC.
All Rights Reserved

41

Verse 2:
Girl, I know that we broke up,
But that doesn't mean you should give the cold shoulder,
'Cuz you know that I really do adore ya'
And that other guy can't do nothing for you, uh, see?
I can tell that you don't really love that guy,
So there's no need for you to go and waste your time.
I think you know I love you more,
Girl, you gotta let him go.
I want you, so just give him the boot.
Call me a hater if you want to,
But I only hate on him 'cuz I want you.
Say I'm trippin' if you feel like,
But you without me ain't right, ain't right.
Say I'm crazy if you want to,
That's true, I'm crazy 'bout you.
You can see I'm breaking down inside
'Cuz I can see you with another guy.
(To Chorus:)

DIGITAL GET DOWN

Words and Music by
JC CHASEZ, VEIT RENN
and DAVID NICOLL

Moderately slow ♩ = 84

N.C.

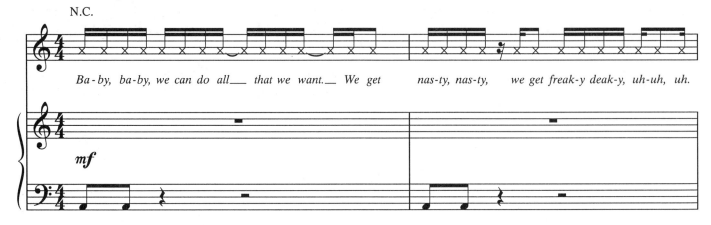

Ba-by, ba-by, we can do all__ that we want.__ We get nas-ty, nas-ty, we get freak-y deak-y, uh-uh, uh.

Ba-by, ba-by, we can do more__ than just talk__ 'cause I can hear ya, hear ya, and I can see ya, see ya, uh - uh.

Ba-by, ba-by, we can do all__ that we want.__ We get nas-ty, nas-ty, we get freak-y deak-y, freak-y deak-y.

Digital Get Down - 8 - 1
PFM0021

© 2000 ZOMBA ENTERPRISES INC., CHASEZ MUSIC and DAVID NICOLL (Pub. Designee)
All Rights on behalf of CHASEZ MUSIC Administered by ZOMBA ENTERPRISES INC. (ASCAP)
All Rights Reserved

Chorus:

Verse:

1. Ev-'ry time I'm sit-tin' home a-lone, girl,___ I can't wait to get you on the phone, girl.___ So pick it
2. I lose my mind just when you're speak-in',___ I see you on the screen I get to freak-in'.___ So get

up,___ babe.___ I can see ev-'ry-thing you do.___
down,___ babe,___ and I'll get___ down for you.___

Bounc-ing me from sat-el-lite to sat-el-lite.___ I love the things you do for me so late at night,___ you turn me
I get so ex-cit-ed when I'm watch-ing, girl,___ I can't wait to see you touch your bod-y, girl.___ It's just

on,___ babe.___ It's like I'm right there next to you,___ yeah.
me and you,___ so we can do what we got-ta do, yeah.___

50

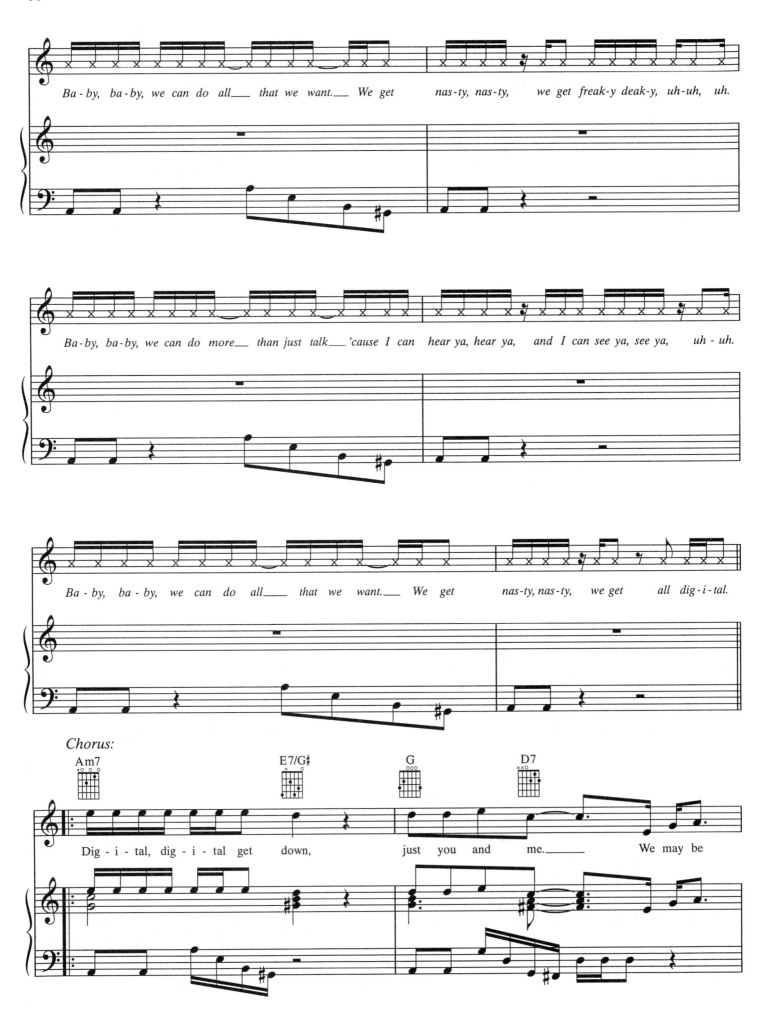

BRINGIN' DA NOISE

Words and Music by
JC CHASEZ and VEIT RENN

Moderate funk ♩ = 108

Bring-in' da noise,___ bring down the house.___ We came here___ to turn the par-ty out.___ Say,

come on, come on, let's raise the roof___ and give 'em proof___ that we can get___ loose, y'all. Bring-in' da

noise,___ bring down the house.___ We came here___ to turn the par-ty out.___ Say,

Bringin' Da Noise - 6 - 1
PFM0021

© 2000 ZOMBA ENTERPRISES INC. and CHASEZ MUSIC
All Rights on behalf of CHASEZ MUSIC Administered by ZOMBA ENTERPRISES INC. (ASCAP)
All Rights Reserved

Verse:

THAT'S WHEN I'LL STOP LOVING YOU

Words and Music by
DIANE WARREN

© 2000 REALSONGS (ASCAP)
All Rights Reserved

59

That's When I'll Stop Loving You - 6 - 2
PFM0021

62

I'LL BE GOOD FOR YOU

Words and Music by
JUSTIN TIMBERLAKE, KEVIN ANTUNES, THEODORE PENDERGRASS,
REGINALD CALLOWAY and VINCENT CALLOWAY

Moderately ♩ = 100

You know I'll be good for you, ba - by.

I'll be good for you.

© 2000 TENNMAN TUNES, KEVIN ANTUNES MUSIC, SONY/ATV SONGS, LLC,
TED ON MUSIC, SCREEN GEMS – EMI MUSIC, INC. and CALLOCO MUSIC
All Rights on behalf of TENNMAN TUNES Administered by ZOMBA ENTERPRISES INC. (ASCAP)
All Rights Reserved
"I'll Be Good For You" contains elements of *"Believe In Love"*
by T. Pendergrass, R. Calloway, V. Calloway, S. Beckman and K. Robinson
© Sony/ATV Songs, LLC/Ted On Music (adm. by Sony/ATV Songs, LLC)/
Screen Gems – EMI Music, Inc./Calloco Music/K. Rob Music Inc. All Rights Reserved

66

I'll Be Good for You - 8 - 3
PFM0021

I'll Be Good for You - 8 - 4
PFM0021

Chorus:

NO STRINGS ATTACHED

Words and Music by
JC CHASEZ, ALEX GREGGS
and BRADLEY DAYMOND

Moderate ♩ = 112

Ba - by, you're not the on - ly one._____

N.C.

Ooh_ yeah,_____ hey_ yeah._

No Strings Attached - 7 - 1
PFM0021

© 2000 ZOMBA ENTERPRISES INC., CHASEZ MUSIC,
ALEX GREGGS PUBLISHING and BMG MUSIC PUBLISHING CANADA
All Rights on behalf of CHASEZ MUSIC and ALEX GREGGS PUBLISHING
Administered by ZOMBA ENTERPRISES INC. (ASCAP)
All Rights Reserved

74

No Strings Attached - 7 - 3
PFM0021

78

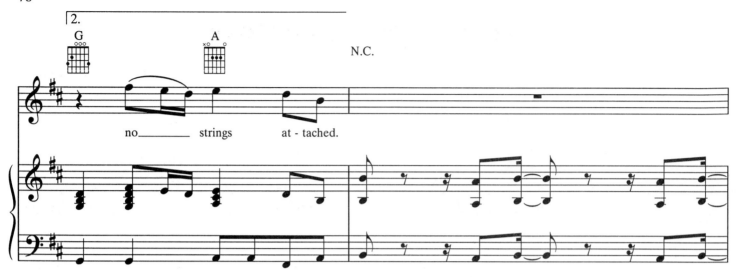

no_____ strings at-tached.

Verse 2:
He doesn't give you the kind of attention
That a girl like you needs, that a girl like you needs.
'Cause he always looks around, his eyes wander 'round.
He doesn't see you like I see, yeah.

Take it from me, it's a lesson to be learned.
Even the good guys get burned.
Take it from me, baby, I would give you love,
The kind of love that you've only dreamed of.
(To Chorus:)

I THOUGHT SHE KNEW

Words and Music by
ROBIN WILEY

© 2000 ZOMBA ENTERPRISES INC./CHICK SINGER MUSIC
All Rights on behalf of CHICK SINGER MUSIC Administered by ZOMBA ENTERPRISES INC. (ASCAP)
All Rights Reserved